GETTING STARTED WITH C#
A PRACTICAL GUIDE

TIM COREY

Getting Started with C#: A Practical Guide

ISBN: 9798987126004

Self-Published by Timothy Corey.

Dallas, TX USA

GETTING STARTED WITH C#
A PRACTICAL GUIDE

TIM COREY

 DevForge

CONTENTS

LETTER FROM TIM

A GUIDE FOR MY FORMER SELF

If I could go back in time, this is what I would hand my younger self. I did not start out as a confident, accomplished C# developer. I started confused, frustrated, and generally lost. I didn't know how to learn C# well, so I did the best I could. I pieced together a learning path full of dead-ends, back-tracking, and frustration. I eventually made it as a C# developer, but I knew there had to be a better way.

This is that way.

You see, every journey needs a map. You need directions to get to each stop along the way. Just randomly wandering around might get you to your goal eventually, but that is far from efficient. If you decide to drive from Lisbon to Moscow, just traveling east would not be enough. Instead, you would map out your route, including major stops along the way.

That is what this guide is. It is a roadmap to becoming a C# developer. By the time you are done reading this guide, you will have a clear understanding of your path to becoming a C# developer, and you will have taken your first step along the path.

So, to my younger self and all those who are like me, follow this path. You will not regret it. Doing so will get you to where you want to be faster and with less frustration.

I look forward to hearing all about your successes.

-Tim Corey

Microsoft MVP, International Speaker, and Software Development Trainer

Texas, 2022

SECTION 1

GETTING STARTED

1.1   WHAT IS C#?

This is a great question to ask right at the beginning. Who wants to learn something only to find out it isn't valuable or isn't for you, right? So let's talk about C# from a high level first.

C# (pronounced "See-Sharp") is a programming language from Microsoft. It is part of .NET, and it is the primary .NET language, but it is not the only .NET language (others include VB and F#). You can use C# to build applications that run on Windows, Mac, Linux, iOS, Android, Xbox, IoT, the web, and more. Basically, if it can run code, it can probably run a C# application. There are few languages with as much reach as C#.

1.2   WHY SHOULD I CARE?

That's great, but can you get a job with C#? Absolutely! There are tons of C# jobs out there. The job market is always a tricky one to read, however. People often tell me there are more jobs for "x" language vs. C# in their area. That may be true, or it may be that there are currently more open jobs for a specific language. The good news is that you will almost always find job opportunities in C#, even if it isn't the most popular language in your market. At the end of the day, you only need one job, not hundreds.

Here is my recommendation: figure out if you like C#. You want to work with a language you enjoy. Being frustrated all day long but having a couple more options when switching jobs is not nearly as beneficial as enjoying what you do. Try C#. If you like it, learn it well.

That is key – learn the language well. Don't just skip around from language to language. Something else will always be shinier or more attractive when you are putting in hard work learning a language. Stick with it. Having depth in one language before you learn another will be key in getting a job. Changing languages too early is like changing your major in college – it slows you down and wastes your efforts. Learning a language well is like getting your degree. You can always get a second degree in a different area, but at least you have your first degree. You can also get more advanced degrees if you want. The choice will be up to you.

So let's get started learning C#.

1.3 SYSTEM REQUIREMENTS

In this guide, we will install Visual Studio 2022 on a Windows PC. A version of Visual Studio runs on Mac, but that has different requirements and configurations. We will save those specifications for the Mac version of this guide.

The minimum requirements for your computer are as follows:

- Windows 10 version 1909 or above (64-bit)

- 1.8GHz processor

- 4GB of RAM

- 850MB of hard drive space

Please note: the above requirements are technically the minimum you need, but the reality is that you will need quite a bit more than that. Here is what I recommend:

- Windows 10 or 11 64-bit (latest version – the edition does not matter)

- Modern processor (this is less of an issue if your PC can run Windows 10)

- 16GB+ of RAM

- 30GB of hard drive space on a Solid State Hard Drive (SSD)

That last requirement might be scary. I understand that. However, remember that you are learning to build enterprise software. You need a tool that will help you do so. You will get many features for that 30GB.

The amount of RAM also seems significant, but the more RAM you have, the faster Visual Studio will run. You will need to figure out how much your time is worth. If you are sitting around waiting for things to load because you don't have enough RAM, it might be worth it to speed your system up a bit.

The good news is that RAM and hard drives are typically upgradeable, even in laptops. They are also one of the cheaper components that you can put in your PC.

If you are going to buy a new computer, or if you are going to upgrade the parts in your computer, here is what I would recommend in order of importance:

1. Solid State Hard Drive (SSD) minimum 256GB
2. 16GB of RAM
3. Second monitor

A second monitor will not make Visual Studio run faster, but it will make you faster. Having a second display will greatly increase your efficiency as you learn. Instead of switching windows from learning to practicing, you can have your tutorial in one window and your practice application in the other.

1.4 INSTALLING VISUAL STUDIO

Let's get this out of the way right away – Visual Studio 2022 Community Edition is FREE! Yep, you can develop commercial apps that you can sell without paying for Visual Studio. Throughout this guide, we will use Visual Studio 2022 Community Edition for everything we do. It is not in any way limited. You will not need to upgrade it later to continue learning. The Community Edition is functionally equivalent to the Professional Edition.

To get Visual Studio 2022 Community Edition, go to **https://VisualStudio.com**.

Meet the Visual Studio family

Under the Visual Studio section, drop down the Download Visual Studio box and select Community 2022.

This will download a small installer to your machine. Once it downloads, run the downloaded EXE file. You may get a UAC (User Account Control) dialog box asking if you want to allow the app to make changes to your device. If you get that dialog box, select "Yes" and continue.

Before the installer can run, it must download the latest information about Visual Studio.

Once the installer is ready, it will present you with a dialog showing which workloads it will install. Let's walk through what to select here and what each item means. But before we do, it is important to note that you cannot mess this section up. Suppose you complete the installation and notice that you are missing items you need. In that case, you can always re-run the installer to add or remove items from your Visual Studio installation. While you should try to get your installation right the first time, feel free to make choices in this next section based on your specific needs.

In the Web & Cloud section, you have four options.

The first is for ASP.NET and web development. This will install several features in Visual Studio that will allow you to work with web projects of various types, including C# web projects. We will select this option.

The next option is Azure development. Azure is Microsoft's cloud platform (a cloud is just a bunch of computers on the Internet that you can use for your applications if you pay the cloud provider). Since Microsoft provides many free cloud resources, and since businesses will be using Azure, we will also select this option.

The third option is for Python development. Python is a programming language not associated with Microsoft. However, they support working with Python applications in Visual Studio. Since we are learning C#, we will not be selecting this option.

The final option in this section is for Node.js development. Node.js is a JavaScript back-end system for supporting web applications. Since we will not be working with JavaScript in-depth enough to need Node, we will not select this option.

That leaves us with a selection like so:

Note on the right that you can see the installation details that we have selected by selecting these categories. You can expand each section to see what additional options you can add if any:

In our case, we will mostly just be selecting the categories and not adding or changing any details. However, we will return to this specific section in a minute to add an additional feature. For now, let's move on.

In the next section, you will see options for Desktop & Mobile.

Desktop & Mobile (5)

Mobile development with .NET
Build cross-platform applications for iOS, Android or Windows using Xamarin. This includes a preview of the ....

.NET desktop development
Build WPF, Windows Forms, and console applications using C#, Visual Basic, and F# with .NET and .NET Frame...

Desktop development with C++
Build modern C++ apps for Windows using tools of your choice, including MSVC, Clang, CMake, or MSBuild.

Universal Windows Platform development
Create applications for the Universal Windows Platform with C#, VB, or optionally C++.

Mobile development with C++
Build cross-platform applications for iOS, Android or Windows using C++.

Mobile development with .NET is all about building iOS and Android applications using a tool called MAUI. MAUI used to be a third-party tool that you had to pay for. Now you get all of the great features of MAUI as part of Visual Studio. You may want to develop mobile apps in the future, so we will install this option. However, if you want to save space, this might be a place to do so.

The .NET desktop development section adds the templates and support for developing three key application types – Windows Forms applications, WPF applications, and Console applications. These will be key in your training, so we will select this option.

Desktop development with C++ allows you to create desktop apps for C++ (makes sense, right?). Just to be clear, C++ is a different language than C#. Since we will not be developing in C++ and there is no reason to learn C++ as a C# developer, we will not be selecting this option.

Universal Windows Platform development is all about creating UWP apps. These are desktop apps built upon Windows 10 APIs (APIs are connection points that applications can use to talk to another system). These are the full-screen (typically) "native" apps you might use in Windows 10. These are important to at least touch upon, so we will be selecting this option.

Mobile development with C++ is similar to the last section; it only uses C++ and does not use MAUI. Since you will not need to learn C++, we will not be installing this option.

That leaves us with a selection like so:

The next section covers gaming.

We will not be making any selections in this category. However, if you are looking to get into C# gaming, the first option (Game development with Unity) is a great way to reuse your C# skills in the gaming field. You can create incredible games using the same syntax you would use at your job to build a line of business applications.

The Game development with C++ section would only be useful if you were learning C++ instead of C#.

To be clear, this is what our selection would look like for this category:

The final section, Other Toolsets, is somewhat of a catch-all for miscellaneous items.

The first option, Data storage and processing, is about working with databases. Since applications almost universally need to store and use data, this is a crucial section to select. When you learn about building SQL Server databases using Visual Studio, it will be essential to have this group of tools installed. We will be choosing this option.

Next up are Data science and analytical applications. If you are getting into machine learning, this might be an important category to have installed. However, for learning C#, it is not necessary to have this option selected. We will not be selecting this option.

Visual Studio extension development is all about customizing and extending Visual Studio. You can create code to make yourself more efficient inside Visual Studio. While this is a more advanced topic, it is something that you may find helpful. We will be selecting this option. However, this is another place where you could save some space if necessary.

Office/SharePoint development allows you to create extensions and modifications to the Microsoft Office products, including SharePoint. Just like modifying Visual Studio to make yourself more productive, you can modify Office to make yourself or others more productive. You can also build apps that integrate with Office products. We will not be selecting this option.

Linux development with C++ is another section dedicated to the C++ language. In this section, you can create applications explicitly designed to run in a Linux environment. Since you will not need to learn C++, we will not be selecting this option.

That leaves us with a selection like so:

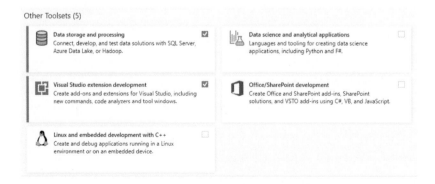

The final thing we need to do is address .NET Framework projects. When .NET was first developed, the system that "runs" our C# code was called the .NET Framework. After 15 years of development, upgrades, patches, and workarounds as technology evolved, the .NET Framework was getting slow and bulky. Microsoft decided to rewrite .NET. The system they came up with was called .NET Core. It "ran" the same C# code as the .NET Framework did, but it was more efficient, had none of the old workarounds or patches, and had some modern improvements, such as running on other operating systems, not just Windows.

Now that they had .NET Core, you would think they would replace the .NET Framework. However, thousands of applications still run on the .NET Framework. So, Microsoft kept both. Today, you can build a .NET Framework project or a .NET Core project. Now that the version of .NET Core has progressed past the last version of the .NET Framework (4.8), we now call .NET Core just .NET. As of the writing of this book, .NET 6 is the latest version. Each year, a new major version will be released.

As a result of this dual set of systems (.NET Framework and .NET), you should be familiar with building projects in both versions. The C# code will not differ greatly, even if the project layouts are significantly different. You should be familiar with both because most companies will use an older version of .NET. Knowing how to work with it will be necessary. Since the differences are relatively minor, understanding and practicing both systems should not be overly burdensome. In the C# Mastercourse, we build projects in both .NET Framework and .NET 6.

For this reason, we need to go to the section on the right, where all our category selections are listed. Under the ASP.NET and web development section, select the ".NET Framework project and item templates" option:

Installation details

- ▾ **ASP.NET and web development**
    - ▾ Included
        - ✔ .NET Framework 4.7.2 development tools
        - ✔ ASP.NET and web development prerequisi...
    - ▾ Optional
        - ☑ .NET Framework 4.8 development tools
        - ☑ Cloud tools for web development
        - ☑ .NET profiling tools
        - ☑ Entity Framework 6 tools
        - ☑ Live Share
        - ☑ .NET Debugging with WSL
        - ☑ IntelliCode
        - ☐ Microsoft Teams development tools
        - ☑ .NET Framework project and item templates
        - ☐ Windows Communication Foundation
        - ☐ .NET Framework 4.6.2-4.7.1 development t...
        - ☐ Additional project templates (previous ver...
        - ☐ .NET WebAssembly build tools

This will ensure that we can create new projects using the .NET Framework.

Now that you have everything selected look in the lower right-hand corner of the window. You should see how much total space this installation will take up. While yours may differ slightly as items are added or updated in each category, the total installation for my selected options comes out to over 27GB.

Remember that I said that 30GB was recommended for Visual Studio? This is why. Yes, that is a lot to install. However, this is an enterprise-level tool that will enable you to get a high-paying job, work for yourself, and/or allow you to retire early. Giving up 30GB of storage seems like a small price to pay, especially when you consider that this is less than 20% of the space taken up by the latest Call of Duty™ game.

Now that you have the Workloads selected let's take a quick trip through the other options in this installer before hitting the Install button.

The first stop is the Individual Components tab:

Here, we can dial in precisely what items we want to be added or removed from our installation. These options have been pre-selected based on the Workloads we selected. We will not be making any changes in this section but familiarize yourself with this section in case you come across a need to have a specific framework, runtime, or tool installed in Visual Studio. This is the place you would find those individual items.

The next stop is the Language Packs tab:

Here you can add any additional languages to your Visual Studio installation—pretty straightforward stuff.

The final stop is the Installation Locations tab:

Here you can change where parts of Visual Studio are installed. This is useful if you want to offload parts of Visual Studio onto a secondary disk. I recommend keeping Visual Studio on your fastest hard drive for the best performance. Note that you cannot change the path to the shared components, tools, and SDKs.

That's it! Now that you have configured your installation, you can hit the Install button. Note that you can install while you are downloading. This saves overall time since it will install as it goes. This is the default, and I would recommend keeping it selected unless you have a specific reason to change it.

Once you start the installation, you will be presented with the Visual Studio Installer:

This installer will give you a real-time look at your progress, including how much you have left to download and how many packages have been installed so far. On the right, it will also give you news articles that you might find interesting to read while you wait.

1.5 STARTING VISUAL STUDIO

By default, once Visual Studio is installed, it will launch. The first time you launch Visual Studio, you will be prompted to Sign in:

Signing in is important. First, by signing in, you will be granted a license to operate Visual Studio 2022 Community Edition. Yes, it is free, but you need to be registered. Second, by signing in, you can store your settings in the cloud. If you log into a different Visual Studio, you can bring in your preferences (font sizes, themes, extensions, and more).

If you do not have a Microsoft account, you can

create one for free. You do not need to use a Microsoft email address. You can use whatever email address you already own and simply register it as a Microsoft account. I recommend you choose this account wisely. If you decide to give up this email address later, you will have difficulty transferring your Microsoft details to a new account.

The next option is to choose your development settings and theme. I recommend you keep your development settings as General, even though there is a C#-specific option. This will change your shortcuts in Visual Studio. Since General is the most commonly chosen option, keeping the same shortcuts as everyone else is easiest. However, this is an option you can change later.

The theme is entirely up to you. These four themes are the four default themes that come with Visual Studio. I prefer the dark theme for daily use and on camera. The reason is that the dark colors stress your eyes less than the primarily white themes. However, for presentations on a projector, I will switch my theme to the Blue theme for better contrast on the projection screen. I will use the dark theme in this guide and future courses.

SECTION 2

OUR FIRST APPLICATION

2.1 CREATING A CONSOLE APPLICATION

Now that Visual Studio is installed, it is time for our first application. It is important to note that practice applications should not "do" anything important except demonstrate what you have learned. Do not attempt to create a "real" application right away. Give it time. Otherwise, you will end up frustrated.

We are going to build a Console application first. A Console application is not visibly impressive but will be quick to create and will not include any time-consuming setup work. When testing what you have learned in C#, it is best to use a Console app whenever possible to shorten your setup time. This gives you more time to do your actual testing.

The first screen you see when you start Visual Studio is usually the "Start Project" dialog (pictured below):

This is where you get started with a project. If this dialog is not open, or if you close it accidentally, you can open it again by selecting Start Window from the File menu in Visual Studio.

On the left are your most recent projects. This is a way to quickly get back into a project you were working on. In our case, we just installed Visual Studio, so no projects are listed yet. There are several ways to get started with a project on the right. In our case, we want to Create a New Project (the last option in the Get Started list).

This brings up the "Create a new project" dialog box.

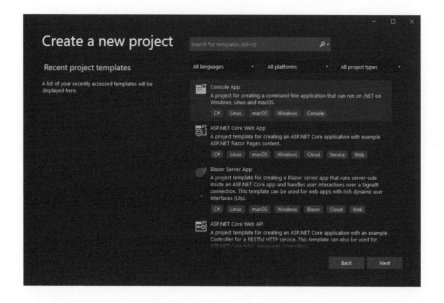

On the left are recent project templates. These are the templates that you most recently used to create projects. This way, if you most often create Console applications, for instance, you could quickly select the Console application template from the left after the first time you used it.

A project template is like starter code. It sets up your application with the configuration and code necessary to get right to work in the project type of your choice. You do not need to use a template. You could manually set up your project from an empty project, but that would be a waste of effort. Project templates handle all of the boilerplate work for you so that you can get started building your actual application.

On the right, you will see a search box, three dropdown menus, and a list of templates. This is where you find the template that you want to use. There are a LOT of them, so we will be using the filter to get us exactly what we are looking for.

To start, select C# from the dropdown on the left. It probably says "All languages," like it does in the screenshot above. By selecting C#, you will filter the templates to list only those that use C# as their language. Remember that Visual Studio can work with multiple languages. By default, even our installation will support VB, for example. Notice that most icons have a small green C# on them. This is important to pay attention to. Some icons will have a blue VB on them instead, indicating a Visual Basic project type. Nothing will work properly if you choose the wrong language template. By filtering to just C#, we avoid these problems.

The next thing we will do is add the word "Console" to the search box at the top. This will look through all of the C# templates (since we are filtering by C#

templates only) to find any templates with the word "Console" in them. Your results should look like this:

Notice that even with both filters on, we get three results and extra results based on our search. WHY CAN'T THIS BE SIMPLE! OK, there is one more thing to talk about, then it should be clear. That is .NET vs. the .NET Framework.

Remember when we had that conversation about .NET Framework vs. .NET Core/.NET 6? This is the "fallout" from that. We have two options: a .NET Framework version of a Console app and a .NET version of a Console app. Which one should you choose?

Choose the .NET version. It is the modern version. The .NET Framework is now only for legacy development.

Don't be scared of the .NET Framework, though. If you see a tutorial demonstrating something in the .NET Framework, that does not mean the tutorial is no longer useful. Remember that almost all C# code is the same from the .NET Framework to .NET Core (and .NET 5+).

One last note about this screenshot: we have multiple options below the line that are "Other results based upon your search". These are results that are partial matches. In this case, they are Console app templates in VB and F#. Do not select templates below that line unless you are sure that the language and framework are correct for what you want.

OK, select the Console App (the first option) and hit Next. That will bring you to the "Configure your new project" dialog box:

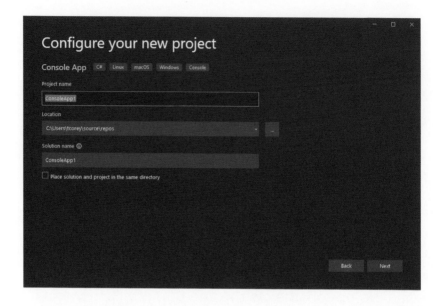

This is where you will configure some essential details about your project. But first, note the tags at the top that tell us where this project can run (Linux, macOS, and Windows). This is just a nice double-check on where you can deploy your application.

The project name will be the name you give your application. Do not use spaces and avoid special characters. This is not a requirement, but it is more of a best practice. You can technically use spaces in the names, for instance, but certain items in your project will be renamed because they don't support spaces. By keeping it to just letters (and maybe numbers), you stick with popular conventions and keep your naming consistent throughout your project.

In our example, we will name our project "HelloWorld". Note that we are using the Pascal case, meaning the first letter of each word is capitalized. This allows you to read the name easily and it conforms to the popular convention.

The project name is important because it will be the root namespace for our application. We will see what this means in a bit. It will also be the name of our assembly. An assembly is a compiled project. For example, a Console app creates an executable (exe) assembly. You can double-click and run this file to execute the application. Other project types create different assembly types (the most common being a dll file). So in our case, our assembly name will be HelloWorld.exe when the application is built.

The next box in our dialog asks us for the Location. This is the location where all of our project files will be stored. Note that when you specify the folder, Visual Studio will create a folder inside it named after the solution (which we will explain in a minute). That means you don't need to create a folder for your project and solution. When in doubt, the default value here will be fine.

The Solution name option allows you to name your

solution. We have already named our project, so what is a solution, and what does it give us? Well, think of a solution as a bucket that we put projects in. Its job is to hold those projects (one or more). That's about it. It is a convenience thing. A solution file does not provide much more than that. It does not provide a link between the projects that are inside of it. It is simply for development purposes that a solution file even exists.

I like to name my solution files differently than my projects. The reason is because the solution (the bucket used for development) is different from the project (the code that will be turned into an assembly). If you name your solution well, it makes it easier to understand what the project(s) inside of it do and easier to look through your solutions to find the correct one. I am going to name this solution "MyFirstProject". Note that the same naming convention and restrictions apply to solutions.

The final option is a checkbox to "Place solution and project in the same directory". I recommend against this. It makes it messier when you add a second project to the solution. I never check this box.

With these options selected, your dialog box should now look something like this:

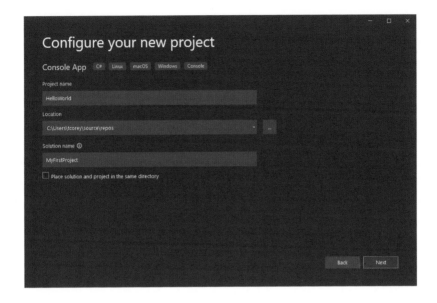

The next screen will ask you to select the correct framework. In my case, I only have one option (.NET 6.0):

As you get new versions of .NET, you will see new options in this list. When in doubt, select the latest version you can. You will note that my version has "(Long-term support)" at the end. This is called an LTS version. Every even version of .NET is an LTS version. That means Microsoft supports it for approximately three years. If you have .NET 5 or any other odd-numbered version, it will say "(STS)" after it. This indicates that it is supported for approximately 15 months from when it is released. All new versions of .NET get released in November. Why this system? Well, companies want stability in .NET. They want major changes every two years. That is the LTS versions. A company can be on .NET 6 when .NET 8 comes out two years later. That company then can spend a year upgrading to .NET 8 while .NET 6 is still supported.

On the other hand, many people (and companies) want changes more often than every two years. As a result, Microsoft puts out major changes in the year between LTS versions. However, supporting these versions for three years as well is an expensive task. Therefore, they support them long enough that support will last at least three months after the next version comes out. If you want to stay on the latest version, you can still be supported during the transition, but it will need to be somewhat quicker (but it is also a more minor upgrade).

One note about support – you do not need Microsoft's support. You can run "unsupported" versions of .NET. The only drawback in doing so will be that if you run into a .NET security flaw or bug, Microsoft will not fix it. They also will not offer paid support of a .NET system running an unsupported version. The application will most likely still operate, in any case.

Let's get back to Visual Studio. Hit the Create button.

2.2 A TOUR OF THE IDE

After a few seconds of setup work, you should arrive at a screen like so:

A LOT is going on here. I am going to explain the important bits. The biggest thing is not to get intimidated by all the options. Yes, it may seem like a lot, but you don't need to use them all yet. As you grow in your C# knowledge, you will learn more of the options in Visual Studio (and it is jam-packed with options). Learning the options as you need them is a much better way of learning Visual Studio than trying to learn the entire editor upfront when you have no context for why things are important.

Right now, my screen is broken up into four major sections. The first is the menu bar/icons at the top. I would recommend that if you need something, look in the menu. The menu has practically everything you need, and it is well-named.

The code section (titled Program.cs) is the work area where you will be doing all your programming. Right now, there is already a bit of starter code set up. This code will help us get up and running, and it will serve as an example to follow to create more code. We will return to the actual code in a minute, but let's finish the quick tour of the IDE first.

On the right, you will see two windows. The top one is the Solution Explorer. This is a view into the structure of your project. It shows you what files are in your project (the entries with extensions – right now we have just one: Program.cs), what dependencies your project has (the external libraries that your project brings in to add functionality to your application), and the overall layout of your files. Note that the solution (MyFirstProject) is at the top level, then there is our project inside of that ("HelloWorld"). Our Program.cs file is inside of our project. This hierarchy lets us know the relationship items have to each other.

The bottom window is the Properties window. This can be helpful for certain applications and situations. If an item has properties (data about the item), the values will be accessible and editable (if allowed) in the properties window.

So that is the default layout of Visual Studio. However, practically everything you see is changeable. For instance, the Properties window is not very helpful when building Console applications. You can click the pin icon in the upper right of the window to get it off the screen. This will allow the Properties window to collapse to just its name on the right. When you want to access the Properties window, just click on the name to see it appear. You can re-click on the pin to keep it open all the time. The Toolbox in the screenshot above indicates how windows look when collapsed.

You can do more than collapse windows. You can drag them to different areas in Visual Studio (the top, bottom, left, right, middle, and more). You can also drag them outside of Visual Studio and use them as separate windows.

2.3 INSTALLING AN EXTENSION

Now before we jump into our code, I do want to modify Visual Studio. You don't have to accept Visual Studio as it is out of the box. You can install third-party extensions (both free and paid) to make the IDE more to your liking. Now, I would highly encourage you to learn to use Visual Studio well before looking to modify it. Too often, I see newer developers sucked into installing extensions and even paying for extensions without understanding Visual Studio first. They end up paying for things that Visual Studio does already.

In our case, we are going to install a font resizing tool. Visual Studio will allow you to adjust practically any font size you want. However, there is not a universal "make everything bigger" option. Instead, you must change dozens of settings. The Font Sizer extension will allow us to make the change once and apply it to all the different fonts in Visual Studio.

To start, open the Extensions menu in Visual Studio:

Select Manage Extensions. This is where you can manage what extensions are installed, add new extensions, and update existing ones that have new versions.

When you select the Online tab on the left, enter "Font" in the search box on the right. Order is important here: ensure you are in the online tab before entering your search term.

The results should be like the screenshot below:

If you want to follow along, select the Font Sizer 2.0 option in the middle and click the Download button. This will download the extension but not install it. Instead, it gives us a note at the bottom that says our changes have been scheduled for after we close Visual Studio.

Once you close Visual Studio, you will get this dialog box:

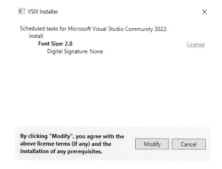

Click the modify button to approve applying the Font Sizer extension to Visual Studio. Now that the extension is installed, we will need to re-launch Visual Studio. If you are on Windows 10, you will probably find Visual Studio in the start menu under Recently

Installed. You can also hit the start menu and type "Visual Studio" to search your installed applications. Once you find the icon, I recommend you pin it to your start menu or taskbar.

When you launch Visual Studio, you will see a dialog like the one we first saw:

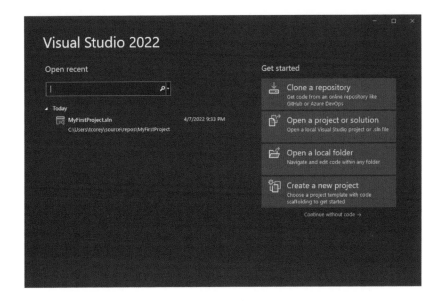

The difference is that under the "Open recent" section, you should see "MyFirstProject.sln". That is the project we just created. Double-click on that entry to open our project again.

Once you are back in Visual Studio, things should look very much the same as we left them. If you installed the Font Sizer extension, you want to enable it. To do so, go to the search box in the upper right corner of Visual Studio and type font:

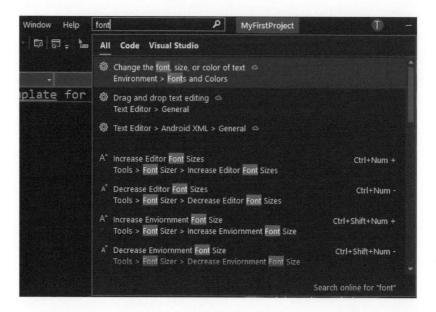

Here you will see options to Increase Editor Font Sizes, Increase Environment Font Size, and corresponding decrease options. You can select an option and then search for font again and repeat the process, which is tedious. Instead, note the shortcuts specified next to each option. You can use these options to change the font sizes rapidly. I increased the editor font sizes multiple times by holding down the control key and hitting the plus key on my number pad. This increased the font for my C# code itself.

Next, I increased my environment font size multiple

times by holding down the control and shift keys while hitting the plus button on my number pad. This increased the font size for most menus and dialog boxes in Visual Studio.

Now your fonts will be easier to read (and easier to see in screenshots). Here is a screenshot of the project once I have applied my much larger fonts:

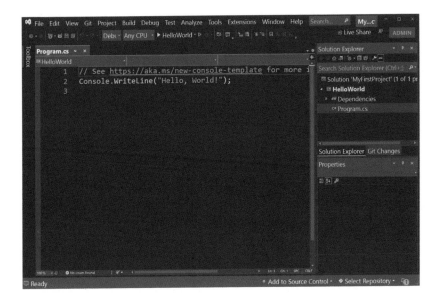

Note how much easier it is to read the fonts in the screenshot. Also, note that some boxes now cut off fonts because the font is too big for the box. You can either play with the fonts to get them to fit without overflowing, or you can live with it. Unfortunately, I will need to just live with it so you can read screenshots more easily.

2.4 UPDATING VISUAL STUDIO

Occasionally, you will see an icon in the lower left of Visual Studio that has a number in a red circle. If you double-click on this icon, it will bring up the notifications for Visual Studio:

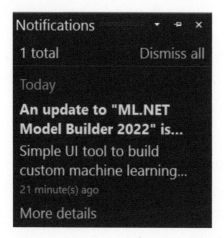

These notifications are typically updates to Visual Studio and the installed extensions. In my case, one extension to Visual Studio needs to be updated. Note that your experience will almost certainly be different since you will have installed Visual Studio at a different time. The basic steps, though, will be the same.

When you have a notification of an update (or

multiple), click the "More details" on one of the updates to open the extensions dialog at the update spot:

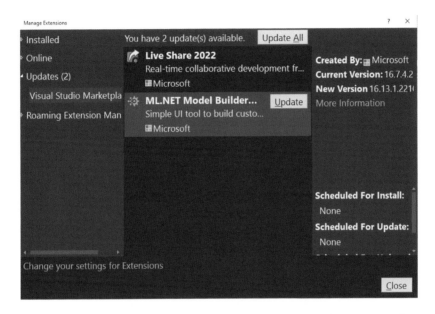

You can also get to this dialog directly by using the Extensions menu and selecting "Manage Extensions". In this dialog, under the Updates section, you can select "Update All" to update all the extensions at once, or you can manually select which ones you want to update. You do not need to update them all. Updates to extensions do not apply until you close Visual Studio. If you have updates, now is a great time to apply them and shut down Visual Studio. Note that even though the initial notification said I had one update, I had two updates.

Once Visual Studio shuts down, the "Download and Install" window will pop up and start installing. Once this dialog is complete, start Visual Studio back up and open the MyFirstProject.sln solution file like before. If it does not open Visual Studio, once the dialog closes, simply open it up manually and navigate to your project. You have now applied all the extension updates.

2.5 UNDERSTANDING AN APPLICATION

At this point, your copy of Visual Studio should look something like this:

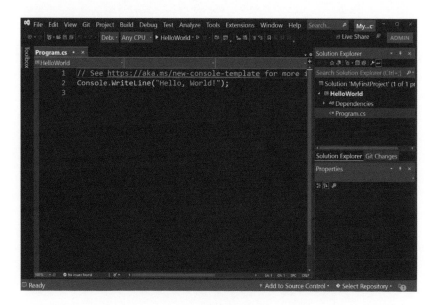

Let's talk about the code that is being displayed on the screen. There isn't much. If you are used to projects before .NET 6, you will feel like a LOT is missing. Now a lot is implied rather than being on the screen. I will go over the various parts you are and are not seeing so you understand what is happening here.

The first thing to notice is the line numbers. Each line of code has a number next to it, including the blank line. This allows us to refer to a line of code easily. For instance, if I said "the code on line 2", you would understand that I am referring to the line that starts with "Console.WriteLine". Note that line numbers do not stay with a given line of C# code. If I added a blank line before the text on line 2, that text would now be on line 3.

Before we get to the actual C# code in our example, I want to discuss how this code works. When we run our application (which we will do soon), the computer needs to know where to start. How does it know which C# code to run first? How does it know when it is done? The answer to these questions is convention. I mean that .NET has a common starting point for all applications. That starting point is the Program.cs file. The application will execute each line of C# code in the

Program.cs file. The application will close when it executes the file's last line of C# code.

That probably seems too simple. How do we have massive applications if only the code in one file is being run? The answer is that most applications call other code in other files from the Program.cs file. In our case, we will not need to do this yet. For now, we will just be putting the code in the Program.cs file.

Now that we understand the purpose of the Program.cs file, life is good, right? Well, yes and no. Once you start writing code in C#, you will realize the Program.cs file is like no other file. We don't have a namespace. We don't have a class. We don't have a method. In every other part of C#, we will need these three items (I'll explain more about each as we need them). Why don't we need them here? The reason is that the Program.cs file is a special file. It is not like any other part of our application, so it looks different. It is as simple as that.

OK, now on to the actual code. On line 1, we see text that starts with two forward slashes. This indicates that this line is a code comment. A comment line is not actual code. It can be any text you want. Typically, comments are used to document a section of code or to share additional information about the code. In this instance, Microsoft included a link to more information about this new type of console template (since it had changed in .NET 6 to this format). Code comments can also be used to temporarily remove C# code from being executed. When your code is turned into an application, the system will ignore the comments in the code. This means comments do not increase the size of your compiled application. Feel free to use them as needed to explain the tricky bits of your code.

Line 2 is actual C# code. The WriteLine is a method. You can tell because an open parenthesis character follows it. A method is a bunch of code that can be used by asking for it by name. In this case, Microsoft wrote a lot of code to write text to a console window. Instead of making you also write that same code, Microsoft wrapped that code up into a package and gave it a name. That package is called a method, and the name is what we use to run that code.

One key principle of learning to write code is DRY. DRY stands for Don't Repeat Yourself. The idea is that instead of re-writing the same code over again, we turn it into a method and call that method as many times as we need. The benefit is that there is less code in your application to maintain, and if there is a problem with your code, you can fix it in one spot instead of fixing it in both spots (and potentially missing one spot). To be clear, DRY can be abused. Not all repetition is bad. You will need to learn the balance over time.

Now you may have noticed that I glossed over the Console in Console.WriteLine. Why do we specify Console? Console is a class. A class is a container that can hold multiple methods (among other things). Every method needs to be inside a class. This allows us to group our methods. Imagine what else the Console class might have. If you can write to the console, you can probably read from it as well. In fact, there is a ReadLine method in the Console class as well.

Note how this notation is written out. Console has a capital "C". WriteLine has a capital "W" and "L". This is called Pascal casing. Every word gets its first letter capitalized. Note that we do not use spaces in names. The capitalization allows us to read the words easily.

This brings up a crucial point. Write this down: code is meant to be read by humans. When you are writing code, keep that in mind. It is not about how few lines of code you can write or how short your method names are. It is about being able to read your code easily. Your code will be read more times than it will be written.

It also touches on another important point: C# is case-sensitive. That means the application would break if you changed the first letter on line 2 from a capital "C" to a lowercase "c". As you progress as a C# developer, you will be confronted by code that does not work. You will probably become frustrated at code that works for the presenter but does not work for you. The first thing to check should be all the little details. Even a single missed letter or letter with the wrong casing can break your application.

Now that we understand that Console is a class and WriteLine is a method, you will see that when we want to call WriteLine in the Console class, we start by specifying the class, and then we put a dot, then we specify the method name. This shows us a clear relationship between the two items. After the method name comes a set of parentheses. That means to call the WriteLine method; the full call would be "Console. WriteLine()". However, note that this is not exactly what we see on line 2. Instead, between the parentheses is "Hello, World!" (including the double quotes). That is what we call a parameter. We are passing data into our

WriteLine method. In this case, we are passing in what is called a string. A string is any text (including numbers and special characters) that we put between double quotes.

The final, essential item to notice on line 2 is the last visible character: the semi-colon. In C#, most lines of code should be ended with a semi-colon. We will not encounter any exceptions to this rule in our demo. The semi-colon tells .NET that a given logical line of code is complete. This means you can put a line break in your code, and it will not affect how it is interpreted. For instance, we could put a line break after the open parenthesis and another before the closing parenthesis, and nothing would break. There would be three physical lines but only one logical line. The way .NET would know that is because of the semi-colon.

When you are writing code, you will invariably forget to include a semi-colon in your code. Visual Studio will start to act weird when you do. Hitting the enter key will not put the cursor in the correct place. You might get red squiggly lines. If you have these issues or are seeing other weird issues, you should first check if you are missing a semi-colon.

Now that we know the various parts of line 2, what does the code do? I am guessing you already know. The console is a text window. Line 2 opens that text window and writes "Hello, World!" (without the quotes) to it. But then what? Remember that .NET will run each line of code in the Program.cs file, and then it will be done. In our case, the application will be done after we run line 2. Let's see that in action.

2.6 BUILDING & RUNNING AN APPLICATION

We want to see our application run (just as it is now). Let's start by opening up the Build menu in Visual Studio.

C# code cannot be executed directly. We need to compile our application. When an application is compiled, the code is converted into something a computer can execute. The build menu is where we can have our application compiled. The first option, Build Solution, will build every project in our solution. In our case, we only have one project, but if we had multiple, all would be built. Building the application means our code gets turned into an executable (since it is a Console application). Below is the option to build the HelloWorld project (instead of every project in the solution).

The next option on the list is the Rebuild Solution action. When you build your application, Visual Studio caches some of the work to make the process quicker next time. The Rebuild action eliminates these caches and starts over to ensure we have all the latest information. If you think you are getting old code or data in your application, doing a rebuild is a good first step in diagnosing the issue.

That is all we are going to cover on the Build menu. The other options have value but are mainly for edge cases and advanced actions. We also are not going to select anything in this menu—the reason is because of the following menu I want you to look at.

Open the Debug menu next. It should look like this:

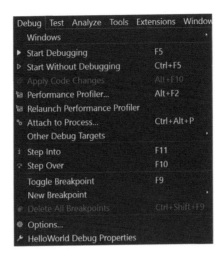

The Debug menu is where we launch our application in Visual Studio. We use this to test out what we are building. The main option I want you to look at right now is the Start Debugging option. This option performs multiple steps. Those steps are:

1. It saves any changes you have made.

2. It compiles the application (the equivalent of hitting the Build Solution option in the Build menu).

3. It runs the compiled application.

4. It attaches the debugger to the application.

Those first three steps are fairly straightforward. We have talked about what compiling does, and running an application is something we do every day. So let's talk about that final step.

When you run an application in Visual Studio using the "Start Debugging" option in the Debug menu (or the equivalent toolbar option), Visual Studio hooks into that application so that you can watch the code run, this allows you to stop the application at any point and inspect what is going on. This is an incredibly valuable option that can be used to troubleshoot problems.

The run mode is the final thing we should discuss before launching the application. This is an option on your toolbar. By default, it will list the run mode as Debug:

As you can see, we can select Debug, Release, or the Configuration Manager. That last one allows us to set up different configurations (like Debug or Release). When developing your application, you almost always want to be in Debug mode. This makes it easier to diagnose issues during debugging. When ready to deploy your application, you want to switch the build to Release mode.

That sounds good, but what does it mean? When we build applications and deploy them to a user's machine, we want them to be as efficient as possible. For instance, soon, we will learn about variables. Variables hold information. A variable named firstName might hold, you guessed it, a first name. Well, that variable takes up memory. In your computer's RAM, a small section is dedicated to holding the value of firstName. But our application does not need to know the value of firstName forever, just until it is no longer needed. In Release mode (the mode optimized for production), once the firstName variable is no longer needed, the memory is reclaimed for other use. That keeps our application's memory usage smaller. However, if you are debugging your application, you might want to know what the value of firstName was beyond when it was last used. That is why, in Debug mode, variables are not destroyed early. It is less efficient from a memory perspective, but it is much better for our debugging needs.

OK, enough setup. Let's launch our application. You can use the play button on your menu, you can use F5, or you can use the "Start Debugging" option in the Debug menu. All of these do the same thing. When you do, you should see a screen like this open:

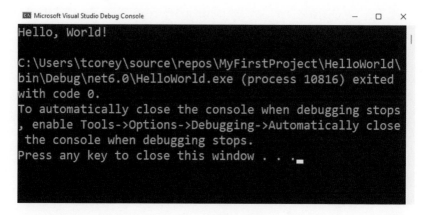

This is the result of our application. As you can see, the first line says, "Hello World!" That is the output from our one line of code (Console.WriteLine("Hello World!");).

After that, you see a few additional lines. Visual Studio generates these to indicate which application ran and to give you a bit of additional information. This is a more recent addition to Visual Studio. Our application was done after it printed "Hello World!" If we were running this application directly, the window would have closed immediately. However, since we were debugging, Visual Studio kept the window open so that we could see the results.

As you can see in the message at the end, you can turn off this feature so that the application behaves like it would in production. We will leave it like it is now. Just note that those are standard lines and not part of our application output.

The window that opens and prints our message is called the Console. It is sometimes referred to as a DOS window by older developers. However, this is not accurate. It is similar but not the same. Despite the simplicity of the view, this is one of the most important user interfaces to learn. I know it is not flashy, and it may even feel ancient, but the console is how we build powerful applications that can be scripted or automated. Web applications in C# are all built on top of the console application. The console is also one of the easiest user interfaces to learn because it requires so little to get started.

This brings up an important note that we need to discuss. No matter what user interface you want to use in C# (ASP.NET, Blazor, MVC, WPF, WinForms, MAUI, etc.), you should start your learning process in the console. You see, those things I listed are user interfaces on top of C#. Just focusing on the user interface is a recipe for failure. Learn the language first in-depth. When you start with the console, you can quickly start writing code. There is not a lot of setup to worry about. That is critical because the faster you can get to writing your actual code, the more practice you will get in the topics you are working on.

For example, let's say you have 30 minutes to practice working with variables. If you create a WPF application to test out your variables, you will first need to set up a textbox and a button on the form. Then you will be tempted to tweak the layout, the font size, and more. Then you need to create the event. Only then will you start thinking about testing what you know about variables. That will take you between 5 and 15 minutes. In a console app, you can immediately start working with variables after creating the project. Let's call it one minute. So, you can create between two and six practice projects in WPF or 30 practice projects in a console app. Which is a better use of your time? Sure, you aren't going to create 30 projects, but if you create between 2 and 5 (my recommendation), you will still have 25 minutes left for your next topic.

OK, back to what we were doing. Close the console window. You can do that by hitting any key or the X in the corner. Either way is acceptable. Our application is actually already closed. This just cleans up our display.

Now let's look at the actual files Visual Studio created based upon running our application. Right-click on the solution file in Solution Explorer and select "Open Folder in File Explorer" (near the bottom):

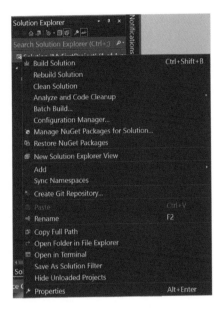

This will open the file explorer at the root of our application:

HelloWorld

MyFirstProject

MyFirstProject.sln

All the files and folders in this folder are part of our application. Note the sln file in this folder. This is our actual solution file. As you can see, it is tiny. That is because it just contains information about the projects inside of it. It does not contain any code. You cannot give someone just this file. If you want to give someone your application, you will need to provide them with the sln file and the HelloWorld folder. The "MyFirst-Project" folder is empty and would not need to be included.

Since we want to look at what Visual Studio created when we built our application, open the HelloWorld folder (note that if you called your project something else, the name of the folder would reflect that project name):

📁 bin

📁 obj

📁 Properties

C# HelloWorld.csproj

📄 Program.cs

The contents of this folder represent all the information about our project. Inside here, you will see a bin folder and an obj folder. These are auto-generated folders. You will not see their content inside Visual Studio. This is where all the files are stored that get built by Visual Studio when we run our application. It is safe to delete these two folders (that is what a Rebuild will do). When I zip up a solution to include as a download, I will go into the zip file and remove the bin and obj folders. This dramatically reduces the size of the zip file and increases the chances that the zip file can be sent via email (email servers do not like exe or dll files in zip files).

In this case, we are looking for the actual application, so we want to open the bin folder. Inside this folder, you will see a Debug folder. Remember that we ran the application in Debug mode. If we had run it in Release mode, we would see a Release folder instead. We could also see both folders if we have run each mode in the past. Open the Debug folder. Inside, you will see a framework folder. In our example, we see net6.0, but you might also see net5.0, netcoreapp3.1, etc. Whatever your folder says, open it. The result should look like this:

HelloWorld.deps.json

HelloWorld.dll

HelloWorld.exe

HelloWorld.pdb

HelloWorld.runtimeconfig.json

These are all of the files created for your application. The most important one, if you are on Windows, is the HelloWorld.exe file. This is your actual application. If you double-click it, it will execute your application directly (note that if you run it, it will launch the console, print the statement, and close the application – there is nothing to stop the application from closing, unlike when we run it in Visual Studio). Since it runs so quickly, you will only see the screen blink, if anything. That's ok. Your application is functioning normally. We will get into how to stop it from closing soon.

The rest of these files each have their own purpose for existing. Just note that while we can execute our file here, when we get ready to deploy the application, we will typically bundle these files into the exe so that it is a much cleaner directory.

2.7 MODIFYING THE APPLICATION

OK, let's get back to the code. We have a running application, but we haven't really done anything yet. We are going to change that now. Start by adding a line return after our one line of code (line 2) and type out "Console." (make sure to put the dot at the end). The results should look like this:

```
2   Console.WriteLine("Hello, World!");                    Solution 'MyF
3   Console.                                             ◢ HelloWorld
        BackgroundColor   ConsoleColor Console.BackgroundColor { get; set; }
        Beep              Gets or sets the background color of the console.
        BufferHeight
        BufferWidth
```

This menu is called Intellisense. Make friends with this list. Seriously. Use it, learn it, love it. Not only does it tell you what options are available, but it also fixes your spelling and letter casing. As you remember, C# is case-sensitive. That means that "console" is not the same as "Console". With Intellisense, you can either click on the suggested item or, if it is highlighted, you can hit tab to fill out the word. This fixes your statement. So, if Intellisense is up, you can type "console" and hit tab, and it will fix it to "Console" since "console" does not exist.

Programming takes great attention to detail. If you open curly braces, you need to close them. If you have two opening parentheses, you need two closing parentheses. Every object name is case-sensitive. Every line of code needs a semicolon at the end (except for the lines that do not). This type of precision can be challenging to do all the time. Intellisense will help you a LOT in making sure you are precise. You just need to rely on it instead of ignoring it.

Let's complete our statement by typing out "ReadLine();" Use Intellisense to fill out the word even if you typed it right. Get used to using it every time.

Your code should now look like this:

```
2   Console.WriteLine("Hello, World!");
3   Console.ReadLine();
```

Console.ReadLine is similar to Console.WriteLine in that it interacts with the console. However, instead of writing data out to the console, it reads data from the console. We can use this to capture information from the user. For example, we can ask for a user's name and then use ReadLine to capture that name. We will do that later. For now, we are using a nice side-effect of ReadLine. You see, ReadLine waits for the user to write an entire line of text. Until you hit the enter key, it will continue listening. That means our application is paused until we hit enter.

Remember how our application closed automatically when we ran it outside of Visual Studio because there was no Visual Studio feature preventing the closing of the window? Well, now the Console will stay open until we hit the enter key. We aren't capturing what the user types. We are just using this to stop our application from closing. That's our first code change.

We have one more change to make to our code. Put a blank line between our WriteLine and ReadLine statements. Type out "cw" and read what the selected option is in Intellisense:

```
2   Console.WriteLine("Hello, World!");
3   cw
4       □ cw                    cw
                                Code snippet for Console.WriteLine
                                Note: Tab twice to insert the 'cw' snippet.
```

As you can see, "cw" is a code snippet. These are shortcuts that will save you a lot of time. A developer has made your life simpler by doing some work for you. In this case, the "cw" snippet will create the following line of code: "Console.WriteLine();" and it will put your cursor between the open and closed parenthesis. All you need to do to execute the snippet and get all this is hit your tab key twice. This will be the result:

```
2   Console.WriteLine("Hello, World!");
3   Console.WriteLine();
4   Console.ReadLine();
```

The snippet created a bunch of the boilerplate code for us and now allows us to fill in the information that will be different every time. Snippets will help you set up common structures as you learn them (such as if, for, foreach, and other statements). This is another way that Intellisense will help you speed up your development and make it more precise without memorizing things.

Now in our case, we want to write a second message to the console. Let's add the text "Enjoy my application" to this second WriteLine statement:

```
2   Console.WriteLine("Hello, World!");
3   Console.WriteLine("Enjoy my application");
4   Console.ReadLine();
```

Note that we now have a yellow border next to the line numbers for lines 2-4. This indicates that we have changed these lines and have not yet saved them.

Once you save them, this yellow line will turn green, indicating that these are newly changed (but saved) lines. This is just one more way that the editor tries to help you identify what is important. If you have one hundred lines of code in your file, skimming through the file and looking for the yellow bands is a quick way to identify where you were making changes.

Let's rerun our application. Now you should see this in the console:

Note that we no longer see the Visual Studio messages at the bottom. That is because we have not finished our application. We are still waiting at the ReadLine method until you hit the enter key. Once you hit enter, it will complete the application, and you will get the Visual Studio message.

Another thing to note is that "Hello World!" is on one line, and "Enjoy my application" is on the next line. That is because we are using WriteLine, which includes a line return at the end of the line. We can use "Console. Write()" instead of WriteLine and it will not add the line return at the end. That, of course, would turn our output into "Hello World!Enjoy my application", which isn't what we wanted. Just note that we have that option. We will be using this option in the next lesson.

SECTION 3

BUILDING AN INTERACTIVE APPLICATION

3.1 DEFINING THE PROJECT

We just learned how to build a simple application. Now let's expand on that information and practice what we learned. In this next application, we will welcome the user to our application. We will then ask them for their first name. Finally, we will greet them by name.

3.2 BREAKING DOWN THE STEPS

When planning to build an application, it is important that your first step is not to open Visual Studio. Instead, break the tasks into steps that you can execute in code. This way, you can identify any flaws in your logic before you have your logic converted into code. Once you have code written, any changes you must make will almost certainly cause you to change your code. Those code changes are where bugs creep in.

To break down what we need to do in our application, the way I see it, we will have about three main sections of code. First, we are going to give the user a generic greeting. This may involve multiple lines of code (and multiple lines on the console), but we know how to do that. That is just WriteLine statements. We can do that.

Next up, we are going to ask the user for their name. This will involve prompting the user to give us their name. It will also involve capturing the name they give us. We have not done this yet. If I were learning this on my own, I would flag this section for learning and practice before we built this application. Since I am teaching it to you, I will teach you what you need to know as we do it. Just note that if you are planning out an application in the future and you identify that there is a section you don't know much about or how it will work, you should learn about that topic and create test projects around that area before attempting to do the work in your real project.

Finally, we will need to greet the user by name. This means using the data we captured from the previous section. Again, I would flag this section as one to practice. We know how to say hello to the user, but we do not know how to use what we have captured as part of that greeting. Saying "Hello Tim" is very different from saying "Hello".

Now that we have the steps broken down (and this is a very simplistic example), we will move on to building our application.

3.3 CREATING THE APPLICATION

To get started, close out your current solution. I find it easiest just to close Visual Studio and open it back up (you won't often be doing this). However, you can also go to the File menu and select "Close Solution". Either way, you should now have an open Start Window:

Note that we now have the MyFirstProject.sln file in the recent solutions list. This will allow you to open your recent projects quickly. You can also pin a project to this list if it is one you will be coming back to regularly.

For our case, though, let's create a new project:

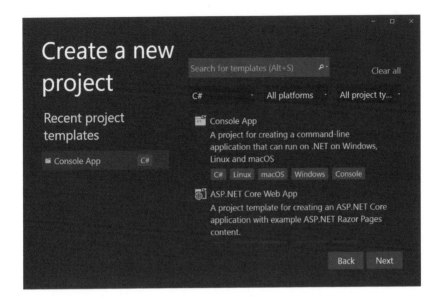

Select a Console App and name the project "GreetingApp". Name the solution "MySecondProject". Place it in whatever directory you want.

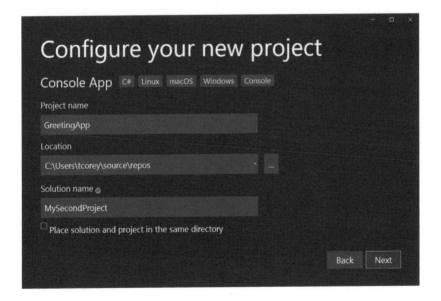

Make sure to choose the latest framework. In our case, that is .NET 6.0:

Now we have our template set up like we had before:

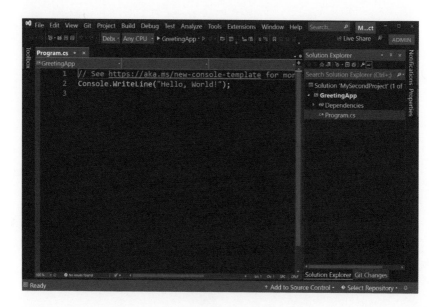

3.4 IMPLEMENTING OUR PLAN IN CODE

Let's start by removing the Console.WriteLine line of code. Now put in four WriteLine statements. In the first, put "Welcome to the Greeting Application". In the second, put "This application was built by ___" and fill in the blank with your name. On the third line, put a bunch of dashes to give us a suitable spacer. Leave the last WriteLine empty. This will just add a spacer line in the console. The result should look like this:

```
2  Console.WriteLine("Welcome to the Greeting Application");
3  Console.WriteLine("This application was built by Tim Corey");
4  Console.WriteLine("-----------------------------");
5  Console.WriteLine();
```

That is one block of code. Put an extra line return in the editor before the next set of lines (still inside the Main method). The editor will ignore blank lines, which means we can use them to make our code more readable without affecting the application negatively (they are taken out when our application is compiled).

In this next section, we will ask the user for their name. We will start with a Write instead of WriteLine. Put the following text inside the parenthesis: "What is your first name: ". Note the space after the colon before the end quote. This will give the user some visual space between the text and where they will be typing.

Next up, we need to declare a variable. As we learned earlier, variables hold information. There are different types of variables depending on the type of data we are storing. For instance, if we want to store a whole number, we would use an "int" (which stands for integer). While learning about the basic variable types should be on your schedule very soon, it is outside this guide's scope. We will learn one variable type, the string type. A string can hold any type of character. It can even hold numbers. The only problem with storing data as a string is that we cannot perform calculations on that data. For instance, if we stored the number 5 as a string, we could not use that string to multiply the value against itself (so 5*5). We would need to convert that string to a numeric type like an int before we could use it for calculations. In our case, this will not be an issue.

To declare a variable, you first state the type and then give the variable a name. So, we want to capture a user's first name and store it in a variable, so our variable declaration line will look like this:

"string firstName;"

Now that we have the variable declared, we can put information into it. On the next line, assign the output of a ReadLine statement to the firstName variable like so: "firstName = Console.ReadLine();"

The result of these three lines should look like this:

```
7    Console.Write("What is your first name: ");
8    string firstName;
9    firstName = Console.ReadLine();
```

Note that on line 9, the Console.ReadLine() code has a green squiggly line under it. This indicates an information message. In this case, it indicates that Console.ReadLine() returns a nullable string (string? vs. string). Strings are always nullable, even without the question mark (which indicates that the variable can hold a null value). This message lets us know that the value we are getting might be null (null means a lack of a value), but our variable is not marked as expecting a null value as a possibility. As we advance, this will make our code better (reducing assumptions). In our case, we do not need to worry about it.

If you are going to ignore these messages, you should turn off this warning. If you ignore information or warning messages, you may miss other messages you do not want to ignore. In our case, we will ignore them, so let's turn off the messages. To do so, left-click on the GreetingApp project file. This will open the project file. On line 7, you will see the "Nullable" line:

```
1  <Project Sdk="Microsoft.NET.Sdk">
2
3    <PropertyGroup>
4      <OutputType>Exe</OutputType>
5      <TargetFramework>net6.0</TargetFramework>
6      <ImplicitUsings>enable</ImplicitUsings>
7      <Nullable>enable</Nullable>
8    </PropertyGroup>
9
10 </Project>
```

Delete this line, and it will turn off the warnings. Just be careful not to delete additional content out of this file. Now, let's get back to working with our code.

After these three lines, add an extra line return before moving on. Next up, we want to greet the person using our application. To do that, create a WriteLine statement. For the text, we are going to say hello, and we are going to use the value of the variable. To do that, since these are strings, we are going to append the two strings together. We can do this by using the plus character. Our line of code will now look like this: Console.WriteLine("Hello " + firstName);

Note that we do not use quotes around firstName. That is because it is a variable that holds a string. It is not a string itself. When the code runs, it will replace the firstName variable with the value it holds. Since this can be different every time you run the application, we now have a dynamic application that responds to user input.

Now put one more WriteLine statement just to wrap up this section. Have it say, "Thank you for using my application". The result for this section should look like this:

```
11   Console.WriteLine("Hello " + firstName);
12   Console.WriteLine("Thank you for using my application");
```

Now just add an extra line and put a ReadLine statement at the end. This will complete our application, which should look like this:

```
1
2    Console.WriteLine("Welcome to the Greeting Application");
3    Console.WriteLine("This application was built by Tim Corey");
4    Console.WriteLine("----------------------------");
5    Console.WriteLine();
6
7    Console.Write("What is your first name: ");
8    string firstName;
9    firstName = Console.ReadLine();
10
11   Console.WriteLine("Hello " + firstName);
12   Console.WriteLine("Thank you for using my application");
13
14   Console.ReadLine();
15
```

Notice how easy it is to read the code since we have those additional lines in the editor. I recommend grouping logical code sections together and then leaving a blank line between them. This makes for code that is much easier to skim.

3.5 EXECUTING OUR APPLICATION

Now run the application and use the name "Sue" when prompted. The result should look like this:

```
C:\Users\tcorey\source\repos\MySecondProject\GreetingApp\bin\Debug\net6.0\GreetingApp.exe    —    □    ×
Welcome to the Greeting Application
This application was built by Tim Corey
----------------------------

What is your first name: Sue
Hello Sue
Thank you for using my application

```

Looking better, right? Now we have an application that interacts with the user, remembers information, and uses that information later.

Congratulations! You have now built two running applications. Now let's talk about how to move on from here.

SECTION 4

NEXT STEPS

4.1 YOUR PATH TO DEVELOPER

I want to start this critical section with the most important thing I can tell you: if you followed along with me and built those two applications, you are now a C# developer. Let me repeat that: you are a C# developer. Full stop. Do not let anyone tell you differently. Not even yourself. Too often, I hear developers say, "Well, I'm not a REAL developer."

Yes, you still have a long way to go as a developer. The thing to remember is that no one was born knowing C#. We all must start where we are at. But once you start, you are a developer. You aren't a professional developer (that takes getting paid for your work), and you aren't a senior developer, but you are a developer.

Now that you have taken a couple of steps down the path to becoming a C# developer, it is time to discuss how to get even further down the path. In the following pages, we will talk about your big-picture path and how to break down each step into individual things to do. We will also discuss the best ways to take these steps and what it means to do this the free way compared to paying for help.

No matter what path you choose or what steps you take along that path, the key to success will always be to practice what you have learned. Software development is not a passive spectator sport that somehow turns you into an athlete. You need to put in the work. Every time you learn something, create 2-5 test projects that ensure you grasp the concepts. The more you practice, the more proficient you will become. Just like an athlete practices their craft before and between matches, you also need to practice your craft to see your best success.

4.2 THE BIG PICTURE PATH

There is definitely an order to learning C#. Certain topics build upon each other. Otherwise, you end up frustrated. For instance, I often have people say they are new to C# and trying to learn ASP.NET Core MVC. That is a tough place to put yourself! Starting there assumes you know object-oriented programming (OOP), variables, classes, instantiation, decorators, extension methods, and a LOT more. Do you feel ready for that? This is why I say that learning C# has a clear order to starting the journey. Once you have reached a certain point, you can branch out, and the path becomes more specific to your situation and goals. In this section, I will lay out for you the big-picture learning path for getting an excellent foundational knowledge of C#.

Each step we will discuss in this section is a large chunk of C# to learn. You will need to break down each chunk into individual topics to learn. In the next section, we will break down the first step into individual topics so you can see how I recommend going about it.

The big picture steps to learning C# are, in order, as follows:

1. Basic syntax commands

2. Learn to debug applications

3. Object-oriented programming

4. Review project options

5. Learn to work with data storage

6. Pick a specialty

7. Focus on that specialty

Let's discuss each step in more detail.

BASIC SYNTAX COMMANDS

This is where you learn about the basic structure of C#. You will learn about variables, if statements, for and foreach loops, do and while, methods, and so on. I recommend doing all this work in console applications.

LEARN TO DEBUG APPLICATIONS

It would be best if you learned how to debug applications as soon as you can write code with any conditionals or branching logic. A significant portion of your career in software development will be spent debugging code. Whether you are trying to get your application to work or fixing someone else's application, knowing how to quickly identify the problem will be critical. Do not skip this step. Do not shortcut your learning by asking for help at the first sign of trouble. Doing so will rob you of the opportunity to learn and grow in this important area. The better you get at debugging, the better you will be as a developer.

OBJECT-ORIENTED PROGRAMMING

This is the big one. This is where you learn about objects, how inheritance works, how to use interfaces and a LOT more. Since C# is an object-oriented language, it is imperative that you really understand how to use the features of OOP. Think of this like going from peddling a bike to driving a car – a big step up but exponentially more power.

REVIEW PROJECT OPTIONS

What is WPF? WinForms? ASP.NET? Blazor? Services? There are a lot of different project types in C#. At this point, you are prepared to understand what each is built upon and how it works at a fundamental level. Get to know the various user interface options, even if you intend to stick with one type of user interface.

LEARN TO WORK WITH DATA STORAGE

Almost every application you create will need to store data long-term. That requires some type of data store. Typically, this would be a relational database like Microsoft SQL or a document database like MongoDB. In general, however, interacting with databases will be similar. Learn how to interact with a few different types of databases, at least.

PICK A SPECIALTY

This is where you identify the course you want to pursue deeper learning. Identify what part of the language and user interface you are most interested in. Identify the items that you want to learn deeper. Test out various options. Research jobs that you might be interested in pursuing.

FOCUS ON THAT SPECIALTY

Create a training plan that will take you deep into your chosen specialty. Learn the intricacies of the subject, not just the easy tutorials. Push your knowledge of the area. Create larger practice applications that combine everything you have learned into a full, working application.

4.3 BREAKING DOWN YOUR NEXT STEP

Your next step is learning basic syntax commands based upon the big-picture path. To help keep you on the right path and moving forward well, we will go over what the topics are to learn inside of this step. That way, you can get help breaking down your first section, and you can gain experience learning the items inside the section. This experience will help tackling the next sections a bit easier.

The topics in this section to learn, in order, are the following:

1. Simple Console app (woohoo! You are done with this step!)

2. Basic variables

3. Conditionals (if/else, etc.)

4. Type conversions (string to int, etc.)

5. Do/while

6. Arrays

7. List<T>

8. Dictionary

9. For loop

10. Foreach loop

11. Methods

For each topic, identify the training source to learn from, go over the material, and then create your 2-5 test projects to verify that you understand what you

have learned. That last step is critical to fully understanding the topic.

4.4 SUCCEEDING ON THE PATH

You have got a great start in C#. You know Visual
Studio, the Console application type, and the starter
C# code better than most developers at your level. This
guide has given you some depth even developers with
years of experience in C# don't always have. Now it is
up to you to take it from here.

You have your big-picture path, you have your next
part of the path broken out into specific topics to learn,
and you know the basic rhythm to learn C#. From here,
you have a choice. You can strike out on your own, or
you can get help.

This is a big choice, where only you can decide the
right answer for your situation. As a developer who
mainly learned on his own but also paid for training
later, I think I have a unique perspective on self-guided
and paid training.

Let me start by acknowledging the obvious truth –
I make money by selling training. That is true. But let
me tell you something else that you might not know –
in terms of content volume, I have one of the largest

YouTube channels. I believe fully in free education. As I see it, you will somehow pay for your education. Either you are going to pay with your money by buying a pre-packaged training plan, or you are going to pay with your time trying to identify the best training resources for the steps you need to take next.

So, let's talk about my paid option. I offer the C# Mastercourse that takes you through big picture step number five. This path that I laid out for you? It walks you through it step by step. Along the way, it also pauses to help you build two larger applications that put all the pieces together that you have learned so far. The final section even works with you on preparing you for getting a job in the real world.

The question is the price, however. Some people tell me that the price is too high. Others tell me that it is way too low. Here is how I recommend evaluating the price and if it is reasonable for you. First, start with the obvious – can you afford it? There are many places in the world where the price is unreasonable. I get that. I also understand that you may not have that type of money available. I strongly recommend against going into debt or endangering your financial well-being to buy this course. You still have the option of paying with your time, and this guide has propelled you down the right path and pointed you in the right direction.

But let's say you could afford the course. Is it a wise choice? I have an exercise for you that will help clarify and ensure you make a wise decision.

Step one – figure out how much your time is worth. Get out a $20 bill (or imagine one). How long would you work to get that $20 bill? An hour? Four hours? Eight? $20 seems like a lot until you consider taking eight hours of your day off to work for it. Then it doesn't sound like enough (at least not to me). Figure out how many hours you would be willing to spend to get that money. Then, double-check your math by figuring out how much money you would make if you worked all day on your day off. Would it be worth it? For example, if you said you would work for two hours for $20, that is $10/hour. That means if you worked eight hours on your day off, you would get $80. Is that reasonable? If not, adjust your hourly rate.

Now, let's figure out how much time a guided course will save you. How much time will it take to identify each step in each section, identify a place to get that training, and then create the test to ensure you understood the topic? Is it ten minutes per step?

Twenty? Let's go conservative and say 10 minutes per step. In the C# Mastercourse, there are roughly 145 lessons (I add content occasionally or adjust the content so this number might fluctuate a bit). So 10 minutes times 145 steps equals 24 hours 10 minutes.

Multiply your hourly rate times the amount of time just finding the topics will save you. If you had said your hourly rate was only $10/hour, that means you would save $240 just in the identifying of the lessons. If you said $20/hour, you would save $480.

But we aren't done. Just saving time identifying the steps and setting up the learning plan isn't the only time savings. In fact, it isn't even the major time savings. You see, I pack each lesson with tons of value. Developers with years of experience take my C# Mastercourse because of how much even they learn. Finding the right training source that won't lead you astray is vital. Piecing together your education will leave you with gaps, where one author assumed you would learn a topic later and another assumed you already had learned it. A cohesive learning plan is worth more than just the sum of its parts.

Being highly conservative, learning from high-quality lessons that fit a cohesive whole is three times as valuable as picking and choosing training. Between the poor trainers, the bad advice, and the hard-to-follow tutorials, it will take you at least three times as long to train on your own. The C# Mastercourse is over 40 hours long. That means training on your own will take you an additional 80 hours at minimum.

Go back to your hourly rate and multiply it by 80. If you estimated even $10/hour, that would be $800. $1,600 if you said $20/hour. But let's say you said that your time was worth minimum wage in the US: $7.25 per hour. With the 24 hours you saved above and the 80 hours you saved here, you will have saved 104 hours of your time taking the C# Mastercourse. That works out to be a savings of $754.

But we aren't done yet – getting done with your training 104 hours earlier means you are applying for jobs 104 hours before you would normally have. Now that doesn't seem like a lot, but when you train for even 10 hours per week, that is over two months earlier. That means you will get a job two months earlier (we are talking in generalities, of course). What will you make at your new job? What will two months' salary be worth? Add that to your savings above.

As you can see, if you can physically afford paid

training and find the right training (not all training is created equally), it is often worth a lot more than you would expect. I would feel entirely justified charging $2,000 or more for the content I provide in just the C# Mastercourse. You will get more software development experience from it than you would a college education. Yet I don't charge that much for the C# Mastercourse. The reason why is because I want you to succeed. I want you to have much more value than you ever pay for. I offer a 30-day money-back guarantee on all my content because I never want a student to question if they got enough value out of my content. I am going to bury you in value.

4.5 CONCLUSION

So, that's it. You've been launched into the exciting field of software development. You have been pointed in the right direction and have your next steps in front of you. Now it is up to you. Are you ready to succeed as a software developer? Are you ready to become who you were meant to be? I can't wait to hear your success story. Just remember that every compelling story has danger, difficulty, and struggle. The key is to keep focused, keep pushing forward, and remember that I am rooting for you. You can do this!

FOR MORE GREAT CONTENT TO HELP YOU BECOME A
WORLD-CLASS DEVELOPER VISIT

IAMTIMCOREY.COM

Printed in Great Britain
by Amazon